IN THE HOOD

A Parenting Pocketbook

A collection of prose and poetry

Parenthood
Motherhood
Sisterhood
Brotherhood

Heather L. Stewart

PUBLISH AMERICA

PublishAmerica
Baltimore

May you enjoy!
HLStewart
2023

ISBN: 978-1-60749-827-8 (softcover)
ISBN: 978-1-4489-9223-2 (hardcover)
PUBLISHED BY PUBLISHAMERICA, LLLP
www.publishamerica.com
Baltimore

Printed in the United States of America

*"I had to be torn down as
an individual
in order to be raised as
an understanding parent."*

IN THE HOOD

A Parenting Pocketbook

Foreword to Parenthood

During our parenting years, we have been complimented, at times, on the behavior or character of our two sons. These are blessed words! Had I ever thought it possible? Not really—or fleetingly at best. Remember, parenthood is easier when strict expectations are absent. Confidence in our skills grows ever so slowly. Learning about the complicated interactions involved between generations is a process. It never ends and, I suppose, it never was intended to end.

We were fortunate to have raised our sons in "Small Town Canada." Everywhere they went, every person they met, was familiar to them. We used to tease them by saying, "be mindful what you say and do, as somebody is always watching!" Sure enough, we received word of where they went even before they came home.

We also encouraged them to see beyond our borders—in reading and in travel. At an early age, they each experienced student exchanges: trips to other countries and cultures, traveled to other cities, provinces and states beyond their 'early' world.

We were told once, at a parent-teacher interview, that our first son was just as what this mother wanted her young boy to grow to be. "How was this possible?" she innocently asked. "How did we raise such a fine young man?" I was stunned.

Was there ever a plan? I had no answer to offer other than, "It took many people of all ages. Neither I, nor his father, did it alone." Faith and hopefulness prevailed.

Our responsibility went only so far. Thinking quietly to myself, I knew in my heart that this was so. And I was very grateful!

Our extended families, our friends and our community, especially our church community, all influenced who he became. What a relief to know! What joyous knowledge to share!

Our second son was not like the first. Why was this a surprise? How did we then learn to relate all over again? The point is, we did. And this time, we knew we didn't know. This time, we were more intimate with the term 'flexibility'. Is he a fine young man? Of course, because he is who he is intended to be. He is bright, caring, creative and spontaneous, of strong character as is our first son—expressed in different ways, as is nature's way.

They follow different paths, but with the same sense of justice, of responsibility, of personal integrity.

Dare I muse that this was all by accident—or by design? Dare I think that what became of them was purely coincidental and that they developed *in spite of* our endeavors?

Do you think this does not pertain to you? Think again, and do read on. Parenthood is definitely a 'trip on the wild side."

Acknowledgments

I dedicate these musings
to our two sons, Jesse and Lucas.
I love you, and I thank you.
We are so very proud of you.

For further inspiration, I joyfully
look to our nieces and nephews
who journey down this path
called parenthood with our
grand-nieces and grand-nephews:
Lily, Aidan, Mackenzie, Ethan, Liam,
Griffin (GG) and Sequoia

God Bless you all!

A Parenting Pocketbook
Lessons Learned

Children are natural, naturally. This is not necessarily so of parents. Parenting is a whole other business.

Parenting has a Purpose.
"Every child is an experiment"

Is there such a thing as a 'natural mother'? I do believe. I think I have actually come close to a few. If we see ourselves as 'one of those', we need read no further. On the other hand, if we think we are doing it all 'right', we are probably wrong.

Am I one? Oh, no. When our two boys came out, each in their own good time—and each with a head the size of a bowling ball, my world was forever reversed: at least for twenty years, or more—their time, of course. For twenty years, I slowly crawled back from that convoluted, crazy ride I'll call 'Mother-mode." It took twenty years for the glaze to clear from my eyes and the haze to lift from my head! If the role of parenthood doesn't leave one feeling drowned in ineptitude, sometimes frozen in fear, there's more.

The rose-colored world of contented mothers with always adoring children is the biggest hoax each generation has ever passed on to the next! Know this, and be armed!

In the beginning, I found it a real fight to 'just break even' with all the mixed messages that society, through various media forms, was offering our next generation. I often said that, "Our former generations had complete influence on their children until those children were at least age five. What a solid foundation!" Now, I was trying to instill basic, solid values while spending too much time explaining the uselessness of advertised products, of the 'more is better' syndrome, of being mean in blocking their supposed desires.

Within their formative years, my mother's generation knew only of the influences within the family home, with farm chores and animals and, occasionally, from a welcomed visitor.

The family's specific ideology was 'stamped' on children as surely as the hot iron branded the cattle. My boys were 'branded' by the brands— products seen on television, heard and talked about among their friends. Many were the talks of essential values, of what distinguishes 'wants' from 'needs'.

Eventually, they grew into a broader mind set of not following what existed, but leading the way in individuality and, thank the Lord, the thriftiness of purchasing at thrift shops.

So, what was it all for? Everything. Everything that, since then, I have come to learn is important: knowledge that can come from no other place. So what does a parent learn? Answer: who I am, of what I am capable: which are my bitterest weaknesses, where are my greatest strengths and, finally, that I do have a limit.

I am eternally humbled!

I have been rolled around so much I can (proudly) say that a few sharp points have been smoothed. I might even say buffed. I am a long way from being a polished gem, but at least I know what to strive for—'Natural Parenting', when love and dedication for a child is unconditional, pure, complete and unwavering.

Did I mention the color rose?

I knew in the bigger scheme of life, and when my boys were either absent or asleep, my heart burst with love for them. It was in the daily, repetitive rituals of discipline and caring, which were constantly being challenged by them, when an inner voice cried, 'enough!"

Dads, in general, focus on actions; Mother's generally focus on feelings. When we parents finally figure this out, we form a more symbiotic relationship. Sometimes he can be soft, sometimes she can be hard.

Keep them guessing—that's my motto!

Toddlers:
What's a Parent to Do?

Potential, potential! Don't like what we're seeing—or feeling? Remember that Mother-mode is a combination of dealing with present moments, while understanding future potential. Toddlers will eventually be civilized. We will eventually feel sane, satisfied, vindicated. Justice does prevail: children do have children.

The eldest boy was big and strong for his age. Taking him to the weekly 'Moms and Tots' group proved to be almost terrifying to me. He just did not understand his own strength when playing with toys and with other girls and boys. The 'terrible twos' is meant to be a time of self-discovery and of declaring one's independence. He and I just did not see ideals in the same way. Add to this a two-years-old negative reaction to me wanting to change his behavior!

I learned then to focus on his potential, not on the reality.

Consistency is the key: even if that means being consistently inept at completing certain household chores, or being consistent in not presenting a home-cooked meal for every dinner. Consistency is a goal but random consistency prevails—in the form of robotic motions from morning to night, day after day, week after week, until that glorious day when they talk. And they talk. They not only tell us what they think, they tell of what we are to think. They thrive on consistency, yet consistently strive to break those barriers.

I remember one time when our youngest, at about age two, completely stunned his father. When his six-foot Daddy glowered over him and told him to, "sit down and be quiet!" the toddler simply plopped onto the kitchen floor at his father's feet. It was some time before he even moved, let alone spoke—even after lengthy coaxing.

They are not like us. They sometimes don't even like us. They are (blessedly) unique—ultimately special.

Do we now remember whatever that was that encompassed our thoughts BC (Before Children?) I think not. We now pull from every weak link of a source about parenting. We find the books. We read the books. We throw the books out. There are no rules—it's a developed instinct that we have to *want* to develop. Not feel natural yet? Ask for help. Not enough? Reach out to the community.

Form a 'Mom & Tots' group. Talk to other adults—they do live beyond our walls.

Remember those wooden carpenter's benches—the ones with colored pegs to hammer through, reverse, then hammer again? This is a great child's toy to redirect aggression. I guess our first son aggressed enough, then swallowed a peg from shear boredom. We didn't know the peg was missing until it arrived in his diapers at the other end! A trip to the doctor ensued with us worrying about colon damage, paint chemicals and how the heck did he do that?! Although we were assured any potential damage had not occurred, we began sharing warnings to all who would listen. Some things are just not meant to happen!

I remember thinking: who are these little people who influence my every thought, every move, I make? Who are these little creatures that seemingly effortlessly suck the energy from my body? They are my sons. They are a whole, new life. They are my island now, in an albeit shipwrecked world.

My sense of responsibility was great, although tempered by moments of shear joy—a hug here, a giving moment there. The shine of shear joy on a child's face when Daddy or Mommy enters the room is gift enough.

See at what they are looking. Hear of what they are saying. Embrace the mountains of spontaneous moments. Once in awhile a serendipitous moment glows so hot that it burns in our memory forever. Those are the gems. (I, who like, or liked, peace and order, found this lesson to be the most difficult.)

When our youngest son was being admonished to improve his behavior— to try harder, at a very young age he looked way up into his father's face and, with hands on hips, exclaimed, "But Dad, this is as good as it gets!"

It's an albeit shipwrecked world.

Have no control—or just feel that we have no control? Of course! All those 'BC' motions to control our world, its material possessions and all who were players in it, no longer exists. Now, if others don't have a four-limbed appendage stuck to their hip, then they no longer understand our world. What? I control feeding time? I control bedtime? I control any time? NO. At this point I no longer control myself. Must sleep. Must eat. Must wash. And, oh yes, I must do it for them, too.

Having pets: be they goldfish, hamsters, guinea pigs or cats and dogs (and I'm sure a few more exotic ones out there) guide the nurturing traits of children. Little ones learn to focus on caring, and loving another living creature. This is good. This leads to not only understanding compassion in themselves, but allows them to recognize compassion from others.

We graduated from the milieu of smaller pets to eventually owning many lop-eared bunnies. Dad even built separate bunny condominiums in the yard where, lo' and behold, three or four quickly became sixteen in number! How did that happen? Too much love? We graduated once again to owning only dogs.

Develop compassion.

Read to our children. Read to ourselves. Then have them read to us. This is a marvelous method to endorse the 'love of learning'. Language and creative ideas go hand in hand. Curiosity and discovery are what make the world such a fascinating place!

It takes a community to raise a child. This could include our church, our family, our neighbors, organized care, but especially friends. Friends understand. Our children's time can be shared. Our *in*sanity can be 'divied up' so it doesn't appear too obvious. Friends are the greatest reflection of who we are. Be good to them. They will be good to us and to our children.

Friends are an anchor.

Take a break. This could be more frequent little breaks weekly, or weekend breaks monthly, or a holiday annually. Take a break! Even the most wonderful experiences lose their lustre if we don't step away for awhile to appreciate their beauty. And this parenthood can sometimes be anything but beautiful.

Taking breaks from our children refuels our energies and balances our lives.

Youngsters:
What's a Parent to Do?

Let go!! I think that is the sole, most significant lesson I ever learned as a parent. Let go. Let go of past concerns, let go of preconceived notions, let go of what others say. Let the world go on without us for awhile. Remember, this is a family island. It is what we make of it.

I found this to be a truly blessed time to rely on my mate, and to discover his reliability. It is surely a time to be vulnerable. I went from feeling I knew what I needed to know to command my world (BC, of course), to feeling like a blithering idiot. My sons even looked at me that way, some days.

In those days of thinking that Halloween costumes and elementary school parades built character and pride in one self, our son later explained to me that, "it was an adult version of child abuse—embarrassing and insulting at best." When I queried him as to what about the leadership skills being formed and the group efforts displayed, he rolled his eyes. I didn't understand. We won't even discuss the apocalyptic maneuvers we went through while helping the boys create costumes—and face makeup— to their satisfaction. We parents each took turns to leave the vicinity of chaos.

I had to be torn down as an individual in order to be raised as an understanding parent.

Many were the times I 'knew' I was making the right decision for the health and well-being of my boys, only to later discover I 'thought' I knew. Their emotional bell-being was not necessarily built on my premises. Their creative choices were theirs alone. I stood aside, aghast! Where did that idea come from?

Be positive. For every negative comment or action, I believe it takes 10 really positive counteractions—just to break even. The more my children saw me interact positively with my spouse, my family, my friends and my community, the more they realized the importance of this. Also, the added love and guidance that others brought to our children was so important, and appreciated. It added to their self-esteem and absorbed into their growing state of self-awareness. So, the more we interacted with our community, and all those within it, and the more our children shared this time with us, the greater the results.

Our eldest son would bring young friends, with seemingly lost souls, home to play. He sensed they were lonely and he wanted to help. He also refused to take part in bullying although he was, at times, bullied: a response, perhaps, from our reaction to his rough 'Mom-and-Tot' sharing days? He felt a keen sense of justice and fair play at an early age.

I have seen both boys offer dialogue and spare change to ones in need— no questions asked.

We can't, and we should absolutely not, raise a child alone.

Our schools hold the ultimate influence in our children's developing years. Be involved in the local schools: visit, volunteer and connect directly to the teachers and principal. This way, mutual respect is developed, issues are understood and any possible negative surprises are met and resolved early.

I learned much about our boys from listening to their teachers. They see a different set of skill sets, character traits and social qualities than we are privileged to witness at home. The reverse is also true.

Our youngest was in a fury during his intermediate school days. He started projects early and strove for perfection, only to sometimes have the entire project rules change or later morph into something else. He spent way too many hours each night in 'getting it right' and, of course, was in tears with tired exasperation. We actually, at times, felt compelled to tell both our boys to, "just do the basic job required and move on to the next." Our meetings with the teachers helped us both to understand and to improve our approach.

Don't let them see us unravel (and we do) in a rather unpleasant craze, as that for sure is the beginning of their doubts in us. Are we who we represent? Can we be counted on 100% perfectly, 24/7 to do the 'right thing'? If not, those young minds now have a tool. Now they see weakness, which only feeds their growing strength. Don't worry. This is good. This gives them a feeling of confidence.

The more we feel drained and dry, the more they are developing.

Take heart. When a parent feels completely used up and emptied, this is because the child has been fulfilled. We have given it our all.

I remember when I was the sole parent at home for long durations, as hubby was on numerous business trips, when I would wait until the boys were away before whipping a wet towel onto the washing machine in great frenzy as I shouted at the top of my lungs. I felt better.

Be non-judgmental. Focus on their actions, not on their character. Avoid opinions, but offer guidance. Clarify expectations and state consequences, then follow through. Reward often. Praise always. Praise all the good and discourage or ignore, if feasible, the bad. Think before we speak. Count to ten, bite our tongues, leave the room.

I remember my husband saying one day, "I've counted to ten at least a hundred times today." Some days we looked hard to find something to praise. Those were quiet days.

Be flexible. If we want our children to complete a chore, explain what it is, then offer a time frame that they may have some control in their doings. Stress the 'share factor' and explain the consequences. I found that, usually, when I made it a personal *need*—to do it *for me*—it invariably worked. Little was accomplished by telling my sons to do something with no added explanation. Be flexible in how they use *their* time. Try to impress balance in all things: more activity requires more food and more rest.

ACTIVITY! Activity! Children are naturally active. Channel this energy. Play or sports, regulated or uncontrolled, help keep their bodies moving. Team sports are also an excellent forum for teaching leadership skills. Encourage participation in various outdoor activities until the child finds one that is preferred. Single person activities, such as swimming, cycling or skiing, are also valuable.

Besides, they sleep better at night, and from that we all benefit.

Once, when our younger son expressed anxiety over not knowing the full route for his first long-distance Track and Field run, in grade five I think, his father told him to simply, "follow the rest." His indignant response was, "But Dad, how am I going to be first if I follow the rest?"

An active body feeds an active mind.

Do boys ever play rough! Tumble and toss is the name of the game. It really doesn't matter what is being tumbled, or who is being tossed. Accidents happen. What a guilt trip that is when our child is hurt while under our care! Under someone else's care and we can feel superior, but *my* child being hurt under *my* care? Others do notice the scars.

I remember being detained for an entire day at the children's hospital while being drilled about child negligence! We skulked home. Our eldest had, by chance, been handling a small bottle of noxious substance, which his father had inadvertently placed within reach while temporarily searching for something else. With tears in his eyes, we couldn't tell if our son had merely sniffed it or tasted it. We went full speed in err of the worst case scenario.

Another time this same boy shoved a bead up his nostril. In trying to remove it himself, he managed to lodge it way up his nose. Little did we know it only takes minutes for swelling to occur. I didn't know emergency health care could produce such long tweezers!

Later, our teenage sons willingly had their bodies scarred: both in the form of tattoos. Plus, the younger son paid to scar his own face in the form of piercings! Broken bones and tiny crutches had also entered our world.

I guess there will always be something 'matcho' about 'sport scars.' From sport scars to sport cars or free-wheeling boards or motorbikes, sons will never leave us bored. Oh, but I am ready some days for shear boredom! I guess this is what mid—to senior-age is all about: a time to rest, a time to reflect. I can't wait.

Take the 'wee ones' to the supermarket and the post office, sure, but also take them to the park and the zoo. Take the youngsters to the museums and the art galleries. Then, later, let them go on their own or with friends to places yet unvisited. Encourage travel and various cultural experiences; the rewards will be returned ten-fold. The more they can figure out on their own, the more reliable and self-reliant they will become. Will they always be safe while dependent, or independent? Not really, so deal with that. No-one is guaranteed a certain life-span or quality of life. Absorb this reality until it feels comfortable.

When our youngest was 10 years old, he decided he wanted to visit his uncle in Toronto—on his own! We boarded him onto the local train, where he was disgusted at having to wear an ID bracelet for the conductor as he proceeded to Toronto Union Station. Said uncle, who was there to meet the boy but not carrying any identification with him, had some explaining to do. By all accounts from our son, this appeared to be the mode of the entire weekend: "I had my wallet but he lost his! I took care of him, though."

Teenagers:
What's a Parent to Do?

Try not to wish our parenting life away. Those first few years seem long but, as each year goes by, they roll together very quickly towards the upper teen ages. As this happens, be aware not to be needed so much. Back off. Listen and prod, as those are our privileges, but do not incessantly poke. Their privacy is tantamount at this stage. Then, ultimately, let go. They will come back—in increments. At this point, that is all our older bodies can take anyway.

As soon as we feel we know 'where they are at', they have already moved on

Talk to teenagers. Seek the appropriate time, then ask the questions, even when little or no response is forthcoming. They at least know we care. Strive to know 'where they're at'— both physically and mentally. How? Watch the outcomes of their endeavors: be they homework, friends' behaviors or a change in personal disposition. Verify where, and how, they spend their time, but do it openly and honestly.

We appreciated that our boys would rather be active or productive based on their own initiatives. We encouraged this. Only so much time 'to do', why sit?

We did not so much censor certain TV programs or electronic games, but were sure to discuss the contents with them. The result was less time spent doing either.

Communication is key.

Teenagers are usually quite reflective about their social roles, peer pressure groups, expectations and personal appearances. Along with this fact is the opportunity for mood swings as they develop at an alarming rate. Our parental role, fitfully and sleeplessly discovered, was not to absorb these deep, personal feelings. They don't ask us to, and neither do they expect us to. Teenagers prefer we didn't absorb their moods into our own psyche, thereby adding even more angst to the teenage trip.

It is hard to love without also hurting.

Be there for teenagers. Be consistent in creating available times in the family home. This helps us to be approachable. Dinner together is a good example: when opportunity exists, discussion prevails. These are also the times to awaken their interests in knowledge and education and to discover their goals.

Our home was a haven for all who would enter. From early childhood through the teen years, we held birthday parties and sleep-overs, then eventually hosted all night couch-floppers. Some mornings, two to six new faces greeted us with a smile. After all, we were there for them. We knew our boys and their friends and where they were, but mostly I think it was because we fed them.

Also, be there when they lead their lives. If this means as a chauffeur to sports, music or meeting sessions, so be it. I found that time alone while traveling in a vehicle with my sons created the most enlightening conversations. Who knew?

Family cottage time or camping time together has been priceless over the years. Without the usual routines or standard concerns, our time together was blessed. We lived as a close unit in a smaller environment.

Our shared experience while surviving the famous 1998 eastern Ontario/western Quebec ice storm is still one of the most cherished memories. Our boys, along with some neighbors, relied solely on us for food and for warmth, and we relied on their resiliency. During those 17 days of no hydro, our little gas fireplace and our gas stove warranted our constant respect and attention. We awoke at dawn and retired at dusk, and together as a family we grew.

Be sure to let them have their space! This means their own physical space where they can indulge in their reflective space. This space is not necessarily going to have the appearance of our choice. It probably shouldn't. It is *their* room, with a chance to express *their* ideas. Slobs and slovenly messes are not to be praised (or cleaned for them), but there exists this pocket of time in every child's development when, "there's just no time,

Mom!" They are on high speed mode. They are not yet ready for the importance of being responsible for oneself. Everything else comes first. When they can't find something important to them (and we do not try to find), they learn to organize, if ever so slowly.

I admit I spent too many years just closing the doors to their self-made messes. When I then heard the question of, "where is my...?" I would patiently think, "It's okay, they are still 'under construction'." As a mantra, I would repeat to myself, "when they move, I will find the corners: when they move, I will find myself" (long ago lost in this ship-wrecked world). I hung onto the day when I would see the light. I actually thought there was something spiritual about that! But it helped.

Learn to pick the battles! We can't always win!

Avoid the word, 'NO'. It is a negative term and it will be received negatively. Many alternate ways, means or times exist, even if it is simply, "I'll think about it." There are those who argue that we parents shouldn't spend too much time explaining situations. I say, "Go ahead, as this will make them better thinkers." Dictating without proof of thought is a lousy way to gain their confidence. Beware, though; we could create a monster of a debater—or philosopher—or lawyer! I say it's worth the risk. If nothing else, it keeps us 'on our toes'.

I have heard it said, particularly with regards to teenagers, that we should respond to those questionable ideas and modes of dress with, "That's nice, let me know how it goes." I believe this is a subtle example of how to remain positive in negative situations. Besides, I'm a firm believer that our children are already 90% developed by the age of 12. Anything we do as parents beyond that just seems, to them, as interference.

Our grown sons are both critical thinkers and effective debaters. The only difference between them is upon which subject they choose to debate, and whether we are in the mood to take part. This is good. They question 'what is' and choose to create 'what could be'.

Remember to say only, "That sounds nice."

Teenagers can easily lose touch with reality if they do not learn their own weaknesses as well as strengths. Help them to accept their own frailties and to learn how to accommodate. By doing so, they will not feel discouraged, but stronger. They will also learn there is no such concept as failure, but as experience, and this is used to move on. In this context, to fail is to be fallible. This is real. May we all fail, then know why. May we parents show by example how to accept ourselves and our shortcomings, not hide behind them. Our teenagers will benefit.

In my years of counseling students with learning needs, one message spoken clearly is that it is most helpful to identify one's disabilities. Students can then address them, understand them and incorporate them as part of who they are—and the sooner, the better. Teenagers then accept themselves as they learn to accommodate. They are then stronger than most: they know how to identify challenges to achieve success. They know how to love themselves.

I tried too hard to present myself as a non-fallible mother. I tried to maintain what I thought my children needed most—a person who showed no weakness. I was wrong.

Teach them how to fail.

Respect ourselves. This can be extremely difficult to do, at times, as we now have a debater/lawyer on our hands. Let our community of friendships help. When we respect ourselves, our teenagers respect us, too: even when they reach a stage of thinking we are always wrong. At least they know for what we stand—in what we believe.

Adult Children:
What's a Parent to Do?

It might seem that now the parenting role can 'cease and desist', but reality is that parenting still exists, yet evolves into a different role. Our communication pattern is built on a different premise. Now, we have respect for the ability of the adult child, while that young adult also feels, or at least seeks, the responsibility for self. There is no specific age as to when this happens, but there are variances in the portions of self-reliance and the timing of pieces of independence for each individual.

I have found that, with my sons, one trait 'jumps ahead' at a younger age, while others develop more slowly. Contrarily, some of these slower traits are exactly what the other son expressed early in development. This may seem obvious, but it is not. Intellectual and emotional maturity arrive on their own terms—no matter how hard we strive to impact.

In most conversations with parents of adult children, the outcome is that we feel they should be a 'complete adult' at a certain age or stage, or upon maturity. I ask, "What is maturity?" Are we not all continuously 'under construction'? It occurs at different times, stages and needs in a young person's life. Yet, either through personal necessity or past perception, we still hold onto this misconception of when independent adulthood occurs. The 'when' may be elusive, but we feel we know 'what' it means: to be free, be oneself, be a contributing member of society, but mostly be paying for oneself/out of the house/self-sufficient. Pick one.

TEA and JAM Theory: overflowing and short-circuited

When did 'twenty-somethings' decide they were old? For how long has our society shifted generations within, seemingly, five-year spans? Every five years seems to bring a new generation of thought, musical tastes, style and ideologies.

I call it the TEA and JAM Theory: some adult children are so full of tea they are ready to explode with stress and anxiety about their world and their place in it. With a myriad of possible life paths offered from endless media sources, critical thinking skills are jammed in the brain circuit until they come to a complete halt. From how many overflowing teapots does it take to 'jam' an individual brain? The awareness of world issues with an overload of facts and information has not necessarily created sound knowledge. Many young adults are now already 'overflowing cups of tea' before they realize from where the tea is poured. Many young adults find themselves discouraged, in denial or depressed.

Many college students who seek counsel barely cope with serious life balancing acts. The burdens they bear are far more complex than most mature adults can manage. These include financial, emotional and mental challenges, which affect academic performance. Even though they are in an educational institution, many are the times when we must come to terms with the fact that academic success is the least of their concerns. Personal health and well-being are first.

Is it our doing—are we parents responsible? Individually maybe: collectively, most assuredly. We know the speed of technology and of human expectations has increased at an alarming rate. We had days before knowledge of world devastation, human violence and 'save the earth' cries.

Our western society unabashedly pushed, prodded and promoted non-essential material goods within every form of media, then un-apologetically created more media devices to expand the rights of consumption and its communication. These last two generations of adult children are expected to incorporate world issues and views, disseminate what is of societal value, while being molded as self-oriented, buy now—pay later, 'throw away and replace' economists. We need not look far in the chain to know the source, and the reason, is money.

Our 'baby boom' generation was protected from violence on radio or television. In the fifth and sixth decade of the 20th century, the newscasts were the most violent programs televised. They even had warnings to parents of non-suitability to young viewers. Consequently, we had little, or no, awareness of the death and destruction from many global conflicts. Those more fortunate among us were raised with a sense of security and belonging within our families and communities. We could simplify our life's purpose to a few specific career goals by emulating those in our immediate circles. We were not aware of the myriad of life pathways available, nor pressured into choosing one gateway at an early age. It seems we were left to develop at our own speed and towards our own comfort zone of employment. We had time on our side: time to reflect, indulge and satisfy our curiosities. This was the legacy from our parents of the war years, many of whom came from nothing and suffered great personal losses during the world wars. They wanted more for us. We, in many ways, want less for our children. We have come to the realization that 'less really is more' for our adult children.

Less really is more.

No generation has grown without its teenage angst, anxieties, insecurities and self-doubt. Today, our concept of time—so little of it, so much to do—moves so quickly that even we parents can easily be 'shell-shocked' as to what is going on around us. Now, our grown children are bombarded with so many facts and sources of information, they are frozen, at times, as to how to use this information, to solve problems, make decisions or think critically.

Do not let the grown children fool us into thinking they are as superb multi-taskers as they appear. Yes, they can talk on a cell phone, keyboard on a computer and stir the dinner pot within the same second, but how effectively? And to what end? For many, their need is to feel much is happening and that it is happening very quickly. But the details are not thoroughly addressed, neither are the prior influences nor past outcomes of their actions. Hours are spent on quick little actions of text-messaging and cyber-spacing—and this is in a world that has placed them 'on hold' for where they quickly want to be next: a self-supporting, yet gratifying employment path.

Don't let the school yard anti-bullying campaigns fool you, nor the anti-disciplinarian, non-consequential approach our 'system' seems to support. Although a positive social message, they camouflage the inherent competitive, me first, mind sets that we've all been guilty of instilling in our youth. Make no mistake that our generation of young adults can be far brighter than any other; they just don't have the prerequisite super-brain to make sense of mass information. Neither do we older adults; we merely return to our prior world thinking and either hang onto the traditional ideologies or go full force into the monetary-gaining race. We need to promote new mentors. They do exist, and we could become one of them.

Parents need to become better mentors.

Even though most parents strive to do well, each child's developing nature and character predisposes that child to his or her own needs and goals based on individual perception of experiences. This becomes more prominent for the adult child. It is obvious to say that no two adults, or children, are alike, yet we tend to emulate words and actions that are common to all parents. Our behaviors do not necessarily meet that child's needs or interests. We express from what we know, and have known by examples. Some children will understand and benefit, while others will not.

Our elder son seemed more accepting of the rituals and reasons within our educational system, and both boys accomplished well academically. However, when our younger son began his first full primary year of school, he stomped home in a fury with the words, "I don't know why they don't tell us what they want us to know in the first few hours, then let us go home!"

He clearly did not accept the conformist approach to individual needs nor abilities. As a result, most of his entire formal education years were spent seeking more challenges within and without the education system, and he quickly grew tired of the existing boundaries so went searching for them on his own. This may be quite common, but it still feeds that disillusionment of when one is supposed to enter, and be part of, this existing societal framework. We do not applaud, nor support enough the creative thinkers. Employers still wish for them to partake of the graduate school buffet of knowledge, as that is our primary proof of their worth—just as the material ownership of goods or the amount of cash in one's bank portrays individual worth in our society. How did we come to this? Is not what one has to offer as a uniquely skilled, hard-working, inventive spirit a requirement for life career success? In some ways the answer is affirmative but, in too many overt ways, the individual assets are non-supported, or worse—they are ignored. And remember, a year in our lives, as parents of adult children, is equal to ten years in a 'twenty-something's' life. Their world rotates at a much faster pace than ours. Their notion of time passage is swift and fleeting, instant and changing.

Within the 18 years of teaching college students, I have noticed the increasing number of second and third career adult students coming back for formal instruction. It is not that they don't know the skills of their trades, but that employers expect, and regulations require, that they earn the official diploma, degree or certification.

Continued personal development and life-long learning is the key to fulfilment, but we should recognize the various ways and means this may happen. Experience and critical thinking skills are best developed outside the classrooms: often times, so is knowledge.

Success comes from within.

Competitiveness has dictated the pathway of instant proof over the proven experience. Add to this the fact that we older 'baby-boomer' generation just seem to not want to let go and embrace change, particularly at the current swift pace. No wonder these young, eager adults are frustrated by the old ways holding onto old expectations. The ones on the perimeter can be the most gifted and most bright, but with an almost compulsive nature, to others with a limited expectation or with an acceptance of methodical development, given their flexible, relaxed personalities. Working hard or having the most potential does not guarantee career success or continued income. Actually, nothing does, and that is another source of anxiety for this new generation of young adults. In the 1950's and 1960's, we feared no loss of job opportunities. Whatever level of education, we felt secure in knowing work was there for us. This sense of security is being lost and is felt as a loss. Grandparents and great-grandparents would understand.

When thinking of security, let us not forget the whopping dollars our society expects in return for a sense of security: vehicle insurance, gasoline, mortgages, life insurance, land tax, purchase tax, and so on, from our young adults. We older generations, gratefully, were afforded the opportunity to evolve more slowly within our society's growing expectations.

As mentioned, I see grown children by the hundreds taking short courses, seminars, certificate programs and applied technical training or apprenticeships. This is good. This develops skills and character. I also notice young adults traverse from one applied seasonal work placement to another. Others travel from one country to another for cultural and learning experiences as temporary work. All this is fine if they feel a sense of accomplishment—of personal growth and preparedness for the next step. What it sometimes masks is the needed awareness of a growing career. Either way, it may waylay the inevitable: the inevitable drive to settle down, have a home, raise a family or focus on specific career development. Many young adults are, instead, not only left on the outside looking in, but are perceived and treated as 'underlings'—feeling small, belittled or even persecuted until little self-esteem is left.

Need we wonder aloud the many contradictions that face our grown children?

In addition, we are constantly reminding this new, young work force—the bearers of our society and its economics, of the global trade and commerce, of the world peace-keeping efforts and disease and starvation-riddled populations, of dire results of climate change, pollution and our collective environmental foot-prints. These seemingly leave little hope for the future.

Embrace hope for the future.

Many young adults WANT to make change—NEED to make change. They are conflicted. They are now aware of necessary change for the benefit of all humanity, but have grown in a generation of 'me and my materialism', while the massive numbers of us in the work force are still not ready, or able, to retire (many due to debt and material acquisitions). We choose to put young adults on hold, to self-train or educate at great time and financial cost, while still being patient about their lives and their future.

Yes, there is great promise in the next decade for our adult youth to explode into employed positions where income will surely happen. What is to be recognized is that they also, as every generation before, yearn to have independent living, transportation and pocket money for non-essentials. Yet, it is a time for limits. Will we parents better influence the expansion of sharing profit to all humanity?

Some young adults try not to think so much, or hide behind excessive alcohol consumption or drug abuse. Some have purposefully placed their ambitions on hold. Others have joyfully found a place in the system, while still others are so keenly aware of this mass of contradictions that they push too hard, or move so fast, the end result is shock, anxiety and disillusionment.

There are those who say grown children of today are enabled, undisciplined and even spoiled. I suppose, given from where we came with our own set of values, we might conclude this. Strappings, beatings and autocratic parents were not uncommon. Many of us were raised to be seen and not heard, and to contribute to family chores before all else. My, how many of us have reversed those old techniques!

We wanted our children to develop self-esteem, join sports or committees, be involved, but we also wished for them to have free self-discovery, times to play and to explore. We just didn't know how to counteract the social pressures, media influences and individual ideals. Volunteering is helpful, but it is not enough.

It is not an ideal world.

Does this grown child specialize in recognizing problems? Is this young adult adept at uncovering all the details of what is wrong, what goes wrong and what can be wrong? If not, some study is required on our part about how to guide solution-focused therapy. We parents need to educate ourselves better. Many effective publications exist, so find one that matches the child's age level or development stage. Mostly, this response to the negatively detailed approach to life focuses on the exceptions: when did you perceive this to go wrong, how did you feel then? What were you doing to make it so? What could we use from that to make this situation better? This method empowers young adults to take back control for themselves. Oh, how important is this sense of control of one's life! Distress and anxiety come mainly from a feeling of loss of control. Teach ourselves and our children how to prioritize, delegate and balance the level of personal expectations. If we believe at all that 'ignorance is bliss', then we may inspire them to understand that simplicity, in its best form, is the path to inner peace and clarity of mind.

Negative Stress is feeling a loss of control: take back control

Simplicity in its best form means the engagement of one's self for the common good, not the common denominator—be this for family, community, humanity or in the workplace. It is a means of 'raising ourselves up' and not pandering to the least common denominator or taking the easiest path. We can now instill in our young adults that less really is more: that 'looking out' is easier, and more productive, than 'looking in'.

Let us all determine that the 'me' in each of us is to focus on the 'we' in cooperative efforts, particularly when it means to sacrifice 'me' yearnings. Our young adults need to know that 'my right' is possible only when we first protect all human rights. It is a moral code.

Simplicity is a goal

To make a choice is to acknowledge there are choices to be made: that options exist from which one can choose. A young adult can choose to take a particular pathway or to focus on the positive more than the negative. Empowerment is in taking the action or making the decision, thereby taking back control. This is not always easy if an adult child is stuck in the TEA and JAM phase or feels that making a choice is equal to making a mistake. So what? Make mistakes, but learn from them. I believe we learn more from mistakes than from when life unfolds as expected.

The saying, "ready-fire-aim" is a good one. It means act, then adjust: not to be frozen with indecision. Go, do, act, discover: whatever it takes, this is the freedom an adult child requires. This is the freedom we parents can acknowledge is their right. No judgments, no opinions. Remember, they have already spent over twenty years with our love and guidance. Allow chances for learning and readjusting on their part. Allow them to know these chances are there for the taking. Support this. Encourage the strength to meet greater challenges, fall, then rise again.

My husband and I had no idea that, when encouraging independence and self-reliance at a younger age, we would raise young adults who felt our expectations were for them to always go forward at the same, formidable pace. When that pace could not be kept, it was easy for them to think that they somehow had failed us or, worse yet, failed themselves. Oh my! We did not mean for them to think of independence as meaning 'going it alone'. We limited the limits, which broadened the consequences—both good and bad—of their own behavior. This is not ideal.

Instill a will to take action: to act is to choose, to act is to exercise will.

It is important to realize that there is no right or wrong, good or bad, method of parenting (when we desire to do well), but that we require an awareness of not just the adult child's response or reaction, but of that child's preexisting perception in the first place. Sound difficult? Not really. Depending on the stage of development from toddler to adult, address the simple questions of why, how, who, when or where. Then listen. This helps develop a base of understanding and of trust in who we are and for what we stand. This is because the topic may be obvious but the viewpoint is not.

Actively listening incorporates the hearing of sounds with the brain mechanisms of grouping and prioritizing while also considering the meaning and feelings behind the message.

I rely on assertiveness by speaking from my own viewpoint—essentially taking responsibility for my feelings and thoughts, rather than on what the adult child should think or do. The conversations among adults are to respect the person and a right to have a viewpoint. I do not have to agree, but to argue is non-productive. Use the words 'you' and 'your' sparingly.

Protect the rights of others, and we protect the right to be ourselves. As a parent, I need to listen more.

Active listening is a precise, developing skill.

We should focus upon listening first, then simply state why we feel and think as we do and stay to the facts or behavior of the other, not the person's humanity or character. Being truthful is not always obvious as there may be more than one truth, but we can strive to be as honest as we can. With this comes integrity which, in short, is to match one's actions and words to one's values. Herein lies the difficulty. Our moral values may be the same, but our life/career values most certainly differ between generations.

Discuss behavior, not personal humanity. The word 'you' should be used sparingly.

Our school system requests life-path decisions be made in junior high years, our society dictates living a fifth to quarter of one's life in some form of formal education or training, our western world media defines our needs and lifestyles…yet, the young adult's sexual desires or mating instincts still develop in mid-teen years, as always. This cannot be, we say, as they are not self-sufficient yet to take on the responsibilities! Then we wonder why so many young adults feel overwhelmed, confused or 'stopped in their tracks'.

While others may not agree, we spoke to our sons of the right to express their sexuality as a privilege, while underscoring the tremendous responsibility. This worked in favor of both generations, as focus was placed on self-respect while respecting others.

We cannot negate sexuality.

Add to this, the queries of the young adult who is bright, articulate, aware, quick and sensitive—those for whom the terms 'patience' and 'gradual' have no meaning. They also feel that rush 'to make one's mark' and develop a solid career base early in life. This generation born from the 1980's to the 21st century are commonly known as the 'why' generation. They have seen much, heard much, absorbed so much more in far fewer years. Inherently, many do see this society as a 'money-grab' and they are not comfortable: they don't like it. They ask 'why'? The unjustified expectations placed upon our grown youth preclude a growing number of young people not fitting our established societal mold. Some adult children are highly stressed, highly anxious and feel segmented from their society and communities. It is imperative that we parents recognize this and act upon it.

We knew, as parents, that we could not solve our adult children's problems, but this, too, is a 'letting go' of patterns set during their childhood years. We could help coach them to overcome issues on their own, we could guide them on problem-solving skills shared in their youth, but ultimately, they must discover how to move from identifying problems to solution-based thinking. This is not easy. Remember the TEA and JAM Theory. Also remember that emotions still overcome intellectual thought—especially for those in their twenties. Be patient, while allowing love and understanding to be shared.

Help young adults focus on what they can control; cultivate optimism and personal power.

If adult children do become lost, try to remind them of the traits, skills and abilities that they already possess. Ask of those times that worked for them and of what they were doing then. Connect to the present so they can gain back a sense of control. Feeling in control is everything. It decreases negative stress, allows for possibilities and reminds us of our worth. Adversity comes to us all at different times, but dealing with adversity is what makes us stronger. It develops a sense of who we are and the strength to go on. Self esteem does not grow when an adult child is enabled, or has others do for him or her; self esteem grows by knowing the difference between 'bad things' happening and the ability to manage these unexpected incidences. It is in knowing the difference between facing a challenge, yet taking steps to overcoming it. Age and experience enable us to do this better. We understand the vehicle bumper sticker which reads, "sh** happens." We know we will go on. The sad truth is that, unless children observe our doing so while growing up, we can't just dictate to them that this is so and expect them to feel better. Young adulthood is a very trying time. Every developing life is an experiment.

Unfortunately, we strove too much to protect our children from adversity: from having to feel badly or deal with negative events. This is no favor. The more adversity they face, the better they become at dealing with unexpected changes. Experience with life-changing events enforces critical thinking skills, which lead to the power to move forward. This is essential for self-control and as measures of controlling our environment.

To enable or protect is to limit self-esteem.

Some young adults absorb feedback from their environment better than others. These are the lucky ones. These are the ones who instinctively know that self-survival is in choosing to use what they learn for personal esteem and emotional balance. They are open to what the universe, or their environment, is telling them. Others feel that what they are experiencing is their own responsibility to the point of fault and that no one else can help or even understand. This adult child is strongly self-reliant, therefore is shocked when disappointment turns inward. The greatest awareness parents can offer is to show by example that we humans are social beings; we support and rely on each other. We need to be needed. We do not stand, and should not try to stand, on our own. Friendship is paramount. One good friend is a treasure. Know that and nurture the intimacy and spiritual uplifting that friendship offers. We may be lone beings, but we are not alone. We may be private or solitary, but we do not flourish in solitude. The giving of ourselves is the greatest gift, but we must allow others to also give to us.

We all need to be needed.

It really is a disservice to raise our children how we think we would want to be raised. It really is faulty to protect them too much from the frailties of this world. The intelligent young adult is now not only fully aware of the casualties of our existence, but is sensitive to the harshness and unfairness.

How do we explain our world? We don't. We encourage the positive, the giving, the sharing and the respect due to one and all.

So, what is a parent to do?

We are to be aware of our role as parent to a grown child's sense of placement or belonging. The struggle between dependence and independence may often be experienced from both perspectives, and quite often at opposing times. Even when we are in agreement about when grown children need to be on their own, we must also redefine what independence really means in the 21st century.

The economics of living as one, the costs and time of further education, the limitations of full-time employment opportunities, the expectations of travel or moving to find employment and the desire on the part of our young people to make correct decisions, not narrow the path, all impede the process. They need to be encouraged to explore, to expand their sense of imminent time and to accept the variations of employment and volunteer opportunities. Mostly, they need to develop a personal understanding of their own strengths and weaknesses and to rely on who they are and what they have to offer as unique individuals. And this they need to do with our blessings and without the pressures of the traditional expectations formed from generations past. From the hierarchy of human needs, our adult children first need to feel secure in supplying their own food and lodgings, then reach out to others for equal measure of food and lodgings, before attaining that level of appreciating their own uniqueness and strengths to offer the society around them, until, finally, a sense of achievement or self-actualization is realized. Time and patience—patience and time are what they need.

Time and patience are what they need.

A Summary of
What I Have Learned

I am proud of my sons. Extremely. I wasn't always proud of my parenting. I felt failure sometimes, but necessity moved me onward. I felt exhausted too often, so I learned to reach out. I felt useless at times, so I forced myself to be useful. I felt misused and abused, but realized those feelings were coming from my own misguided expectations, not from any intent on their part.

I did learn so much. I realized that I was not the only person in their world. There were many more. I chose a mate wisely (and with measure of good luck). I learned to choose my friends and neighbors wisely. Then, I learned to give up and give in as to what was solely 'my way.' Although Mother-mode may, indeed, be a serious purpose, I strove to not take it so seriously. Children grow naturally, if we don't interfere too much. They need our love and our support, but not always in obvious or overt ways. This, too, is a continuous balancing act.

Mother-mode is not a competition. Sometimes, we tend to

feel as rivals with our own children. We strongly feel an urge to 'win this case'. This 'us versus them' syndrome easily evolves, but it is not necessary. We are all experiencing the same shipwreck, remember, on this island called a family. Our children, no matter the size, are *equal* human beings. With this knowledge the opportunities already exist to find common ground. Strive to be happy in what we do. Focus on this goal.

Unlike a merchandise order from Sears, we cannot send our children back for a refund. Neither can we trade them in. We can only change ourselves, in how we respond to them. We seek help, admit shortcomings and know that it is okay to sometimes feel ineffectual as a parent. This shows we still care, that we are still conscious.

For those of us who feel we are not born to be parents, Mother-Mode is a process of finding our way. We never really arrive, we merely, somewhat, get used to the trip. If we are lucky, we embrace it. The ultimate reward is to know we have finally accomplished something in these most tumultuous times. Parenthood encompasses the greatest 'highs' and the deepest 'lows'. This is because our love is so strong and our fear of potential loss is so great. In adversity we grow. Our children not only survive, they thrive. The marathon has been won. They are now free to be contributing members to their society and to themselves.

Do all adults need to join this marathon, called Parenthood, in order to be fulfilled? Decidedly not! Beware the danger—we do change! Mother-mode does equal 'overload' in much of our current society. Forgive ourselves; this is not our fault.

There, I believe the hoax has been exposed.

The two boys face each other while at the cottage many years ago.

Son reflecting while standing on the window seat of our old stone home

Foreword to Motherhood

"There is no greater satisfaction than to touch someone's heart through acts of compassion and words. My mother taught me this."

This poem was written at age 25—long before I became a parent. I gave it to my mother the year she became a widow and lost her role as wife. I guess I wanted to emphasize that she still was held dear as a mother.

She hung it on a wall in her home—framed and all!

It reflects my image of my Mom, and her ideals.

No wonder it was so difficult to fulfill my own expectations of parenthood!

Mother has been gone nine years now, but I did take the opportunity to share this during a Mother's Day, Christian Family Sunday service on the first Family Sunday in May after her death, in honor of her life.

It was well received, and many people expressed afterwards that it brought tears to their eyes—for all mothers, living or no. This was good. This touched some hearts.

This poem received honorable mention in a Poetry Institute of Canada competition.

When Thinking of Mom

Visions of Mothers combine all that is good in the ups and the downs of Motherhood.

Mother means 'nurture'—to help us to grow
into one of those people we'd all like to know.
Mother means 'heart' that is made of true gold,
that is molded and burnished as the years unfold.
A heart that expands as the years goes by
with a seemingly endless source of supply
of the love and the warmth she so freely gives
to those who surround her as long as she lives.

Mothers create a comforting nest
of wide open arms, where you go for a rest
from your thoughts and your moods, when you're happy or
low, a Mother is 'home' and that's where you go.

From the days when she taught you to pray on your knees,
    to be kind and polite and to always say, "please":
    where you ran as a child when you were distressed,
    who knew that an ice cream meant sheer happiness.

A Mother can see what no words can explain;
    she knows where you've been, if you're sad or in pain.
You always know her guidance is there
    when it seems there is no friend left to care.

She knows your mistakes, your faults, imperfections,
   but always has faith to guide your direction,
   and gives you the freedom to do it your way,
   so you can say, "I am me, and I know it," some day.

A Mother means 'giving' in true sense of the word:
   of her time, love and self, to the rest of the world.
The only time 'take' is a part of her day
   is when she so wants to take pain and sadness away.
If only Moms knew it. Do you think that they do ~
   know each day of the year is a Mother's Day, too?
Do you think that they know MOM means "I love you"?
I hope my Mom knows that I do, I sure do.

With love always, Heather

Forward to Sisterhood

I wrote this piece over twenty years ago for my only sister to present to her on her 35th birthday. She and her husband were, by then, parents of two young daughters.

We siblings of two boys and two girls were raised in a Royal Canadian Air Force family, so subsequently were moved many times. Because of this, I always looked to her for guidance, and she (usually) provided it—God Bless her!

Sisters, especially when only two, create a bond that only life's end can break.

I believe the details tell the story of many a sister and of many a family's relationship.

For Marlene

Marlene Rose was born one fine seventh day of May
    in the city known as Ottawa, not so very far away.
    She was chubby as an elf, with blonde curls for all to envy:
    like an Air Force Shirley Temple, she came to be a lady.

Through thirteen moves,
    some serious thought, a lot of love and caring,
    she learned to be our sister, and for us she learned the sharing
    of her time and toys and toil, and even of her room,
    and found it's fine to be late bloomers when it means you
finally bloom.

Remember waiting to grow up,
    to finally leave your home,
    be a woman, have a job, lead a life of your own?
    To be free and independent—yourself for to find
    and leave a busy household and those hassles far behind?

Then along came Bobby, looking for his 'blondie':
    he had an image of his woman and her style.
    He knew what he wanted, and he knew it when he saw it,
    for he found his missing piece in your smile.

Then life began in earnest with a hubby and a house,
    with a job of teaching children what they were all about.
    The two of you together to lead a life, you thought,
    then came Shannon and Miss Jennifer, and everything they
brought.

You made a house for two into a family home
  with decisions and more moves to make to find more space
to roam.
    With job transfers, responsibility, came a change in life,
    from a child, then a teacher, now a mother and a wife.

You will grow with grace and style, that we all can see,
  as you use your time and talents to raise a family.
  The children, they will grow and be women on their own
  and will dream the dreams you had not so very long ago.

But the biggest challenge given for each person to surpass
  is to know what is around you that brings true happiness.
  A woman is not a woman until thirty years of age.
  Marlene, you've just begun to start *your life* on its first page.

The day will come when we will long to be thirty-five again:
  to know that youthful sweetness, when womanhood finally came.
  It was a dream of the future, now present, eventually past,
  but each challenge met and remembered is what will make
it last.

Pioneers we'll *all* be, some future distant day,
  with creaks and groans, our hearing aids on, and our hair a
pepper grey.
    But we'll sit back in our comfy chairs, each in our own way
    and think of our young and restless years, as on our Thirty-
Fifth Birthday.

Love to you always,
Heather

Foreword to Brotherhood

My brother, Doug, is my one surviving brother. He is very dear to me. As a sculptor and artist, he travels to many countries for inspiration.

Many years were spent in PietraSanta, Italy, where he sculpted marble. Time was also spent on Vancouver Island sculpting western red cedar.

He has hosted many Art Shows, here in Canada and abroad. His most notable work was as part of the team creating the Canadian national "Adult Survivors of Child Abuse" monuments in Toronto, and a five foot tall penguin in yellow marble—now in Germany.

He was then commissioned to sculpt a large garden portico for the new University of Ontario, a science and technology university in Durham County.

I wrote this poem as a letter to him after he moved to Italy, when our father, who questioned his pursuits, passed away.

I had missed him. I wanted to express how I felt.

I think it did the job. I can only hope that all siblings identify.

What Is a Brother?

What is a brother, if but a man
who lives his life the best he can.
What is a brother, if you ask, "of whom?":
he belongs to the world, though of the same womb.
A brother holds love, he breathes life and laughter
for those he is born with, and those met thereafter.
He is an enigma, a brief thought to hold,
though he exists in himself, as a fern to unfold.

A temple, at times, to compare your reaction:
a child at times, with quiet compassion.
A much maligned fellow, who, in his own way
is making a statement—a sign of the day:
which, in itself, is a trial to win
what with the questions of friends and of kin,
who wonder where peace of mind enters in
when your battleground lies on a platform thin—
of the wants and the needs we think we require
as we stand on our firmness not to inquire
of what lies beyond our basic desire.
Therein lays the stuff of our soul-searching fires.

A wondrous sentiment—that of a brother,
who is nurtured and cared for by the same mother,
and therefore a comrade to share goals that are met,
with not the same loss of truths or regrets.

To be so intertwined as the tendrils of vine
is a bittersweet taste, but one that's all mine.
If I just please to choose it and vow not to lose it,
I know I will have it: you are there when I need it.
That bond that dependency cries to be rid of,
yet so precious to me the stuff you are made of.
Imperfections of freedom you fight so to keep,
if for but a chance to sow and to reap
a taste of the wine that proud confidence brings;
you applaud the creation, as simple birds sing.

If for each step forward you twice stumble back,
then your break from the normal is not what you lack
But if for each stumble you've nowhere to fall,
then being a sister means nothing at all.
My wish for you, Doug, are the moments to measure
those aspects of life that for you are the treasure
of each day, what it brings, how you feel, what you do,
for the world is a village for someone like you.

Love to you, Heather